WAFFLE

Chris Raschka

A RICHARD JACKSON BOOK • Atheneum Books for Young Readers   NEW YORK   LONDON   TORONTO   SYDNEY   SINGAPORE

Atheneum Books for Young Readers

An imprint of Simon & Schuster Children's
Publishing Division

1230 Avenue of the Americas
New York, New York 10020

Book design by Chris Raschka and Ann Bobco

The text of this book hand lettered by Chris Raschka.

The illustrations are rendered in acrylic and ink with brush.

Printed in Hong Kong

10 9 8 7 6 5 4 3 2 1

Library of Congress Cataloging-in-Publication Data

Raschka, Christopher.

Waffle / by Chris Raschka.—1st ed.

p.   cm.

"A Richard Jackson book."

Summary: A child who is always worried finds a way to
overcome his fears.

ISBN 0-689-83838-7

[1. Self-confidence—Fiction.] I. Title.

PZ7.R1814 Waf 2001

[E]—dc21   00-037124

FIRST
EDITION

To Paul

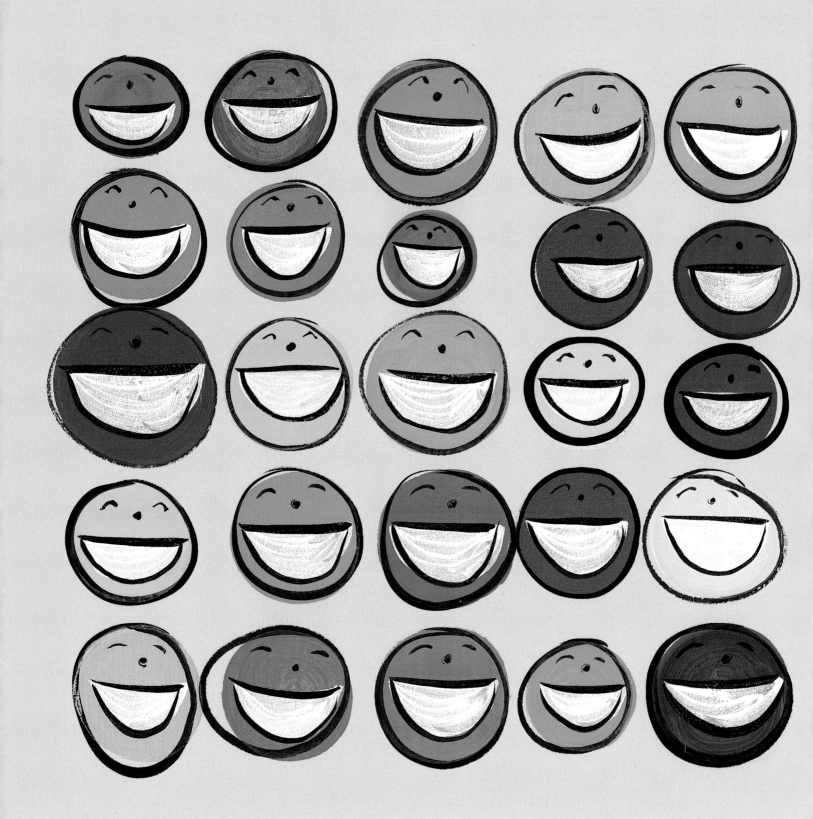

WAFFLE
WORRIED.

WAFFLE
WIGGLED.

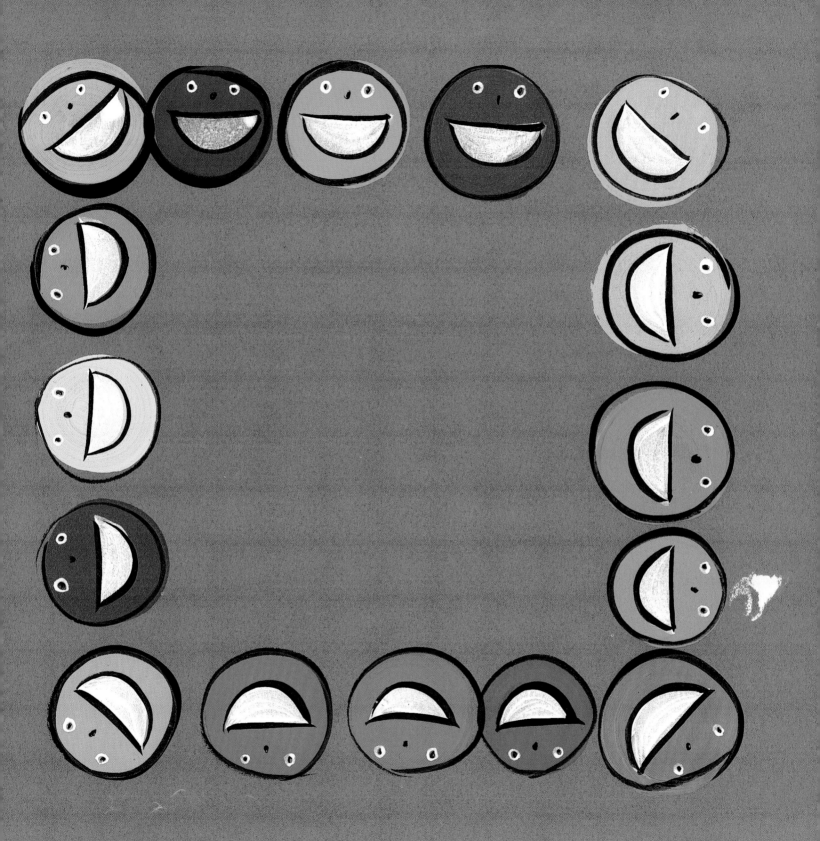

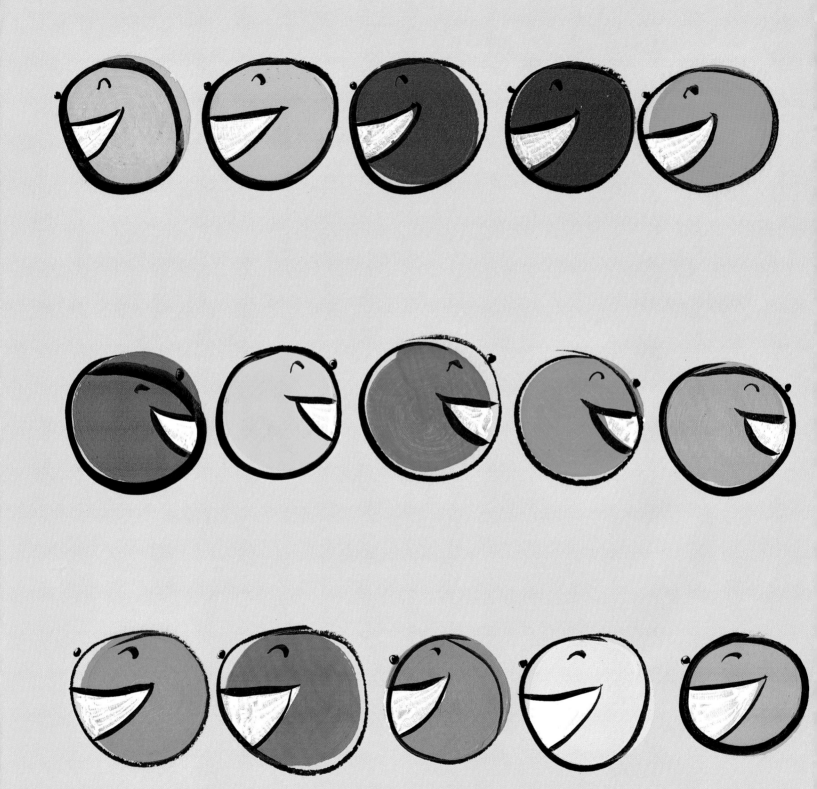

WAFFLE
WONDERED
WHAT IF —

WAFFLE
WISHED THAT HE
WOULD —

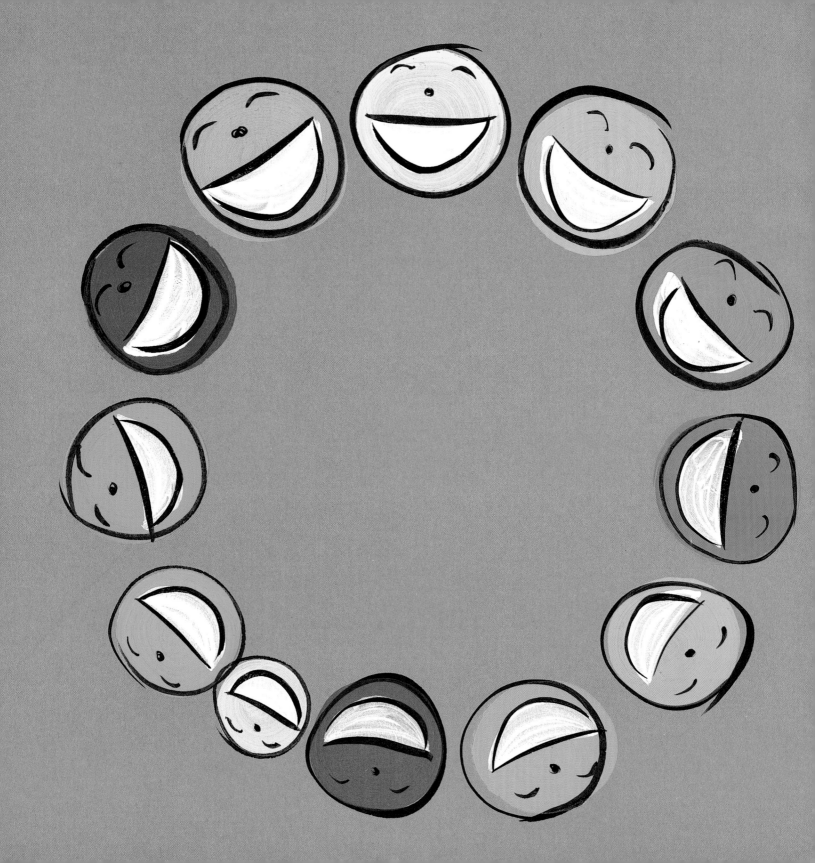

WAFFLE
WANTED TO,
WELL —

WAFFLE

WOULD IF HE

WERE —

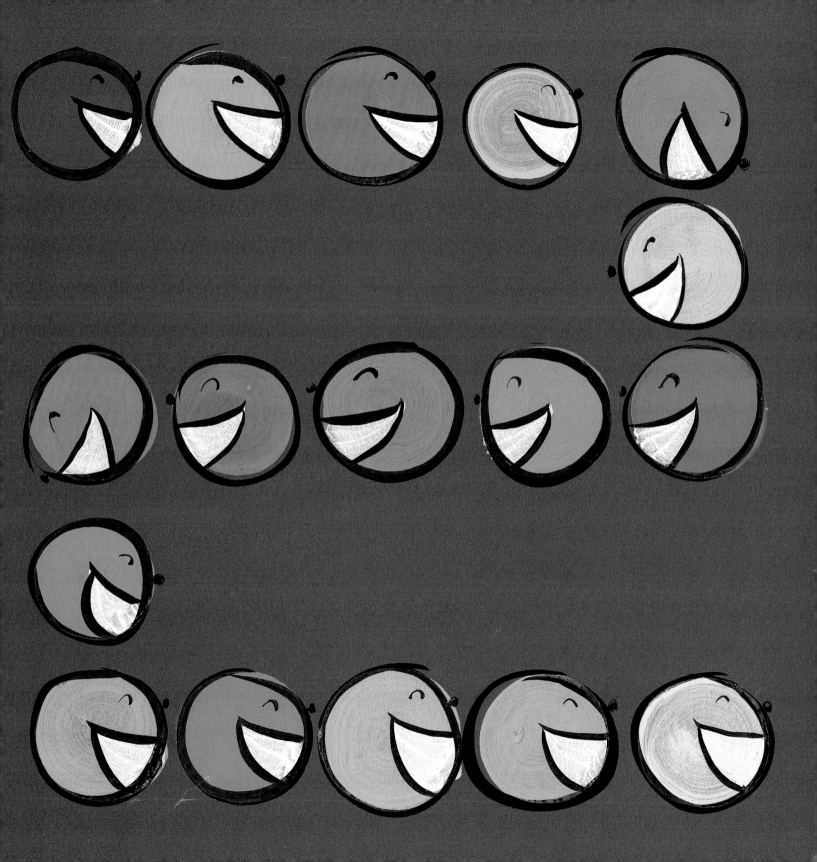

WAFFLE
WOBBLED.

WAFFLE
WAFFLED.

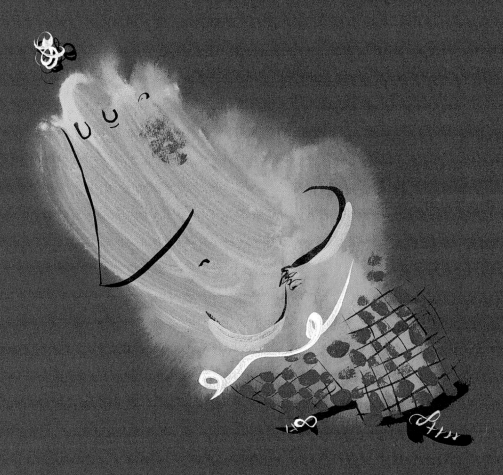

WAFFLE
WAFFLED. HE FELT
AWFUL. HE
WAS A
WAFFLER AND
WAFFLERS
WAFFLE.

WAFFLE WAFFLE WAFFLE

WAFFLE WAFFLE WAFFLE

WAFFLE WAFFLE WAFFLE

WAFFLE  WAFFLE

WAFFLE WAFFLE

WAFFLE

WAFFLE

WAFFLE

WAFFLE

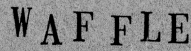 WAFFLE

WAFFLE WAFFLE WAFFLE
WAFFLE WAFFLE WAFFLE

WAFFLE WAFFLE WAFFLE
WAFFLE WAFFLE WAFFLE

WAFFLE WAFFLE WAFFLE
WAFFLE WAFFLE WAFFLE

WAFFLE WAFFLE WAFFLE
WAFFLE WAFFLE WAFFLE
WAFFLE WAFFLE WAFFLE

WAFFLE WAFFLE WAFFL
FFLE WAFFLE WAF FLE WA
AFF L E WAF FL E W
WAF FLE WAF FLE WAF
E WAF FLE WA FF LE WA
LE WAFFLE WAFFLE WAF
WAFF L E W AFF LE WAFFLE
A FFLE WAFF LE W A FLE
WAFFLE WAFFLE WAF
A F F L E W A F F
FFL E WAFFLE WAF

FLEW

FLEW.

WAFFLE FLEW.

NOW
WAFFLE
FLIES,
STILL A LITTLE
FEARFULLY
BUT

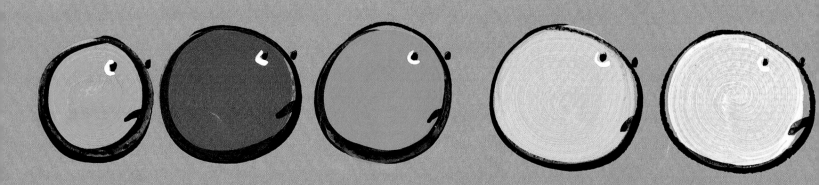

WAFFLE
WORKED
A WONDER
(WITHIN).